TELL THE TALE

BY ABBY BADACH DOYLE

THE TALE OF SLEEPY HOLLOW

Enslow PUBLISHING

INVESTIGATE!

Please visit our website, www.enslow.com. For a free color catalog of all our high-quality books, call toll free 1-800-398-2504 or fax 1-877-980-4454.

Library of Congress Cataloging-in-Publication Data

Names: Doyle, Abby Badach, author.
Title: The tale of Sleepy Hollow / Abby Badach Doyle.
Description: Buffalo, New York : Enslow Publishing, [2024] | Series: Tell the tale | Includes bibliographical references and index.
Identifiers: LCCN 2023010134 | ISBN 9781978535497 (library binding) | ISBN 9781978535480 (paperback) | ISBN 9781978535503 (ebook)
Subjects: LCSH: Irving, Washington, 1783-1859. Legend of Sleepy Hollow–Juvenile literature. | Ghosts–New York (State)–Sleepy Hollow–Juvenile literature. | Headless Horseman (Fictitious character)–Juvenile literature. | Sleepy Hollow (N.Y.)–Legends–Juvenile literature.
Classification: LCC PS2067 .D69 2024 | DDC 813/.2–dc23/eng/20230316
LC record available at https://lccn.loc.gov/2023010134

Portions of this work were originally authored by Shalini Saxena and published as *The Legend of Sleepy Hollow*. All new material in this edition is authored by Abby Badach Doyle.

Published in 2024 by
Enslow Publishing
2544 Clinton Street
Buffalo, NY 14224

Designer: Tanya Dellaccio and Claire Wrazin
Editor: Abby Badach Doyle

Photo credits: Series Art (leather background) Rawpixel.com/Shutterstock.com, (paper background) Daboost/Shutterstock.com, (metal plate) maxstockphoto/Shutterstock.com, (explore more background) Didecs/Shutterstock.com; cover (Headless Horeseman) HelloSSTK/Shutterstock.com; cover (background) Manbetta/Shutterstock.com; p. 5 Daniel Eskridge/Shutterstock.com; p. 7 (map) File:Nearctic-Northeastern_United_States.svg/Wikimedia Commons; p. 9 benoitb/iStock; p. 11 File:Ichabod_Crane_Schoolhouse.jpg/Wikimedia Commons; p. 12 File:What_fearful_shapes_and_shadows_beset_his_path_-_The_Legend_of_Sleepy_Hollow_(1899),_frontispiece_-_BL.jpg/Wikimedia Commons; p. 13 andreiuc88/Shutterstock.com; pp. 15, 19 courtesy of the Library of Congress; p. 17 File:MU_KPB_019_The_Legend_of_Sleepy_Hollow_-_Illustrated_by_Arthur_Rackham_5.jpg/Wikimedia Commons; p. 21 Sunny Celeste/Alamy Stock Photo; p. 23 File:John_Quidor_-_Ichabod_Crane_Flying_from_the_Headless_Horseman_-_1948.68_-_Yale_University_Art_Gallery.jpg/Wikimedia Commons; p. 25 KenWiedemann/iStock; p. 27 Mason Barden/iStock; p. 29 (bridge) Nick L/Shutterstock.com, (Sunnyside) Kenneth Sponsler/Shutterstock.com, (church) Brian Logan Photography/Shutterstock.com, (statue) James Andrews1/Shutterstock.com, (Sleepy Hollow cemetery) Wirestock Creators/Shutterstock.com, (compass rose) Kashtanowww/Shutterstock.com

Printed in the United States of America

CPSIA compliance information: Batch #CSENS24: For further information contact Enslow Publishing at 1-800-398-2504.

CONTENTS

Words in the glossary appear in **bold** type the first time they are used in the text.

A SPOOKY STORY

The **legend** says Sleepy Hollow isn't an ordinary place. The people of the village know it is filled with spirits and ghosts. But one ghost is scarier than them all . . . the Headless Horseman. He is a body without a head who rides his horse at night!

"The Legend of Sleepy Hollow" is a short story written by American author Washington Irving. Since it came out, it's become a favorite spooky tale. Many movies and TV shows have been made about Sleepy Hollow and the Headless Horseman.

EXPLORE MORE!

Washington Irving wanted his story to be scary but a little funny too. Even if you haven't read the story, you might recognize the Headless Horseman from Halloween decorations. Often he is shown with a pumpkin as his head.

"The Legend of Sleepy Hollow" was first printed around 1820.

A QUIET TOWN

The story begins in Tarry Town. It is a quiet village on the Hudson River in New York State. Many Dutch settlers lived there before the **American Revolution**. "Dutch" is the name given to the people of the Netherlands, a European country. Near the village is Sleepy Hollow. It is misty, with woods and a stream.

In real life, Washington Irving lived in the Hudson Valley. He knew the area well. There is a real village called Tarrytown there. Another town renamed itself Sleepy Hollow years after the story came out.

EXPLORE MORE!

The Headless Horseman was said to be the ghost of a soldier. He fought against the colonies in the American Revolution. A cannonball took off his head. At night, he rides from the graveyard to the battlefield to look for his head.

WHERE IS THE HUDSON VALLEY?

The Hudson Valley area is 150 miles (241.4 km) long.

ICHABOD CRANE

Sleepy Hollow is spooky at night but normal during the day. It has one school and one teacher, Ichabod (ICK-uh-bahd) Crane. He moved to Sleepy Hollow from Connecticut. This makes him different from the other villagers. Most people who live there were born and raised in Sleepy Hollow.

Ichabod is a firm but fair teacher. He doesn't make a lot of money, though. He teaches singing lessons. He also helps townspeople with chores, such as farm work and babysitting. During the year, Ichabod lives with the families of different students.

EXPLORE MORE!

Ichabod Crane shares his name with a type of bird. Their appearances are alike! Cranes are tall birds that live near water. In the story, Ichabod is very tall and thin. He has long arms and legs and a beak-like nose.

Ichabod Crane is a schoolmaster, or a teacher who is a man.

DO YOU BELIEVE IN GHOSTS?

Like many people in Sleepy Hollow, Ichabod believes in supernatural things. He loves to share ghost stories and other spooky tales. Ichabod really loves a book called *History of New England* ***Witchcraft*** by Cotton Mather. He almost knows it word for word!

In the evenings, Ichabod often sits and visits with the older women of the town. He tells stories he knows about witchcraft. He also listens to their tales of ghosts, haunted places, and other things. Of all the stories, the Headless Horseman scares and delights him the most.

EXPLORE MORE!

Supernatural means unable to be explained or seeming to come from magic.

In the time of Ichabod Crane, school was held in a one-room schoolhouse. In this type of building, students of all ages sat together. These schools were once very common, but now very few remain.

AFRAID OF THE DARK

Ichabod loves spooky tales, but he is afraid of the dark! After an evening of telling stories, he walks home alone at night. In the dark woods, his eyes and ears start playing tricks on him.

The chirps of birds and toads sound extra scary at night. Each bush looks like a ghost. Every burst of wind sounds like the howling of the Headless Horseman. The sound of his own footsteps makes him jump. To feel brave, he sings songs he knows from church.

EXPLORE MORE!

The Headless Horseman was said to be a Hessian soldier. Hessians were soldiers from an area called Hesse-Cassel in modern-day Germany. About 30,000 Hessian soldiers helped the British fight the colonists during the American Revolution.

Even the flashes of fireflies scared Ichabod on his nightly walks.

IN LOVE

Ichabod wants to marry a woman in town named Katrina Van Tassel. She is the daughter of a rich farmer in the town, Old Baltus Van Tassel. As an only child, Katrina will **inherit** her family's money one day.

Katrina is pretty, but Ichabod has other reasons to want to marry her. He is always hungry, and her father's farm has lots of fine food! Ichabod thinks of all the tasty things he could eat if the farm was his. He could enjoy roasted pig, juicy ham, tasty sausages, and more.

EXPLORE MORE!

During this time, other men are also trying to win Katrina's love. This is called courting. To spend time alone with Katrina, Ichabod gives her singing lessons twice a week. They sing and then take walks at sunset.

Katrina has rosy cheeks and dresses in fine fashion.

BROM BONES

Another man courting Katrina is named Abraham Van Brunt. People call him Brom for short. He is sometimes called Brom Bones because he is large and strong. He is also a bit of a bully.

Ichabod is the opposite. He is quiet and stays out of trouble. He wants Katrina's love, but he doesn't want to fight with Brom. He knows Brom would win if they got into a fight. Instead, Brom and his friends play mean **pranks**. They ruin Ichabod's schoolhouse and tease him in front of Katrina.

EXPLORE MORE!

Brom Bones stuffs up the schoolhouse's chimney so it blows smoke inside. He flips the furniture upside down. Ichabod thought witches did it! Brom even trains a dog to whine loudly. He uses the dog to make fun of Ichabod's singing voice.

Other women like Ichabod, but he likes Katrina the most.

BIG NIGHT OUT

Brom and Ichabod continue to fight over Katrina. She won't choose between them. One fall day, Ichabod is teaching. He receives an invitation to a party at Baltus Van Tassel's farm. He grows very excited—a chance to win Katrina once and for all!

Ichabod goes home to get ready. He dresses in his best clothes. He wants to fit in with the other guests. He borrows farmer Hans Van Ripper's horse, Gunpowder. The horse is old, slow, and blind in one eye. Still, he hopes it **impresses** Katrina.

EXPLORE MORE!

Ichabod looks pretty silly riding Gunpowder the horse. The foot straps fixed to the saddle are too short for his long legs. His bony elbows stick out to the sides, like wings. Washington Irving writes that he looks like a grasshopper!

Ichabod spent extra time getting ready.
He wore his only suit.

DANCE THE NIGHT AWAY

The first thing Ichabod does at the party is eat all the delicious food. He fills his plate with dinner and sweets. Then the music starts. Ichabod dances with Katrina. He is not a good dancer, but he doesn't know it. He is having too much fun to care!

Later, guests start telling ghost stories. Ichabod tells tales of witchcraft from Cotton Mather's book. People talk of seeing the Headless Horseman in Sleepy Hollow at night. Brom brags that he isn't afraid of the Horseman. He says he even raced him once.

EXPLORE MORE!

When Ichabod gets to the party, Brom is already there. He rode his own horse named Daredevil. No one else can ride Brom's horse. It is too strong and fast. At the party, Brom is jealous watching Ichabod dance with Katrina.

At the party, Ichabod is sure Katrina will marry him.

A BROKEN HEART

As the party comes to an end, Ichabod is sure he has won Katrina's heart. He speaks with her before he leaves. But things do not go the way he planned. She only spent time with Ichabod to make Brom jealous. Ichabod is heartbroken. He leaves the farm and rides off into the dark woods.

Ichabod's fear of the dark comes back. He thinks he sees ghosts. He passes a spooky tree. He stops before he crosses a bridge over a stream. The locals say bad things have happened here.

EXPLORE MORE!

The spooky tree existed in real life. This giant tulip tree had big, twisted limbs. It was known as Major André's tree. Major André was a military leader in the American Revolution. Locals said bad spirits haunted it!

Ichabod whistles to himself as he travels home.

THE HEADLESS HORSEMAN

Ichabod sees a strange shape hiding nearby. The shape begins to move. His worst fear has come true. It is a headless rider—with his head in his hand! Ichabod tries to escape, but the Headless Horseman is right behind him.

Ichabod thinks he can make it to the church bridge. As he approaches, he sees the rider rise up. Then he throws his head at Ichabod! Ichabod tumbles to the ground. The next day, all that remains on the road is Ichabod's hat. Next to it is a smashed pumpkin.

EXPLORE MORE!

In the stories the townspeople told, the Headless Horseman could only ride so far. He always disappeared before crossing the bridge near the church. When the Horseman reached the bridge, he would vanish into flames.

Ichabod thinks he feels the Horseman's hot breath on his neck!

NEVER SEEN AGAIN

The next morning, Gunpowder the horse turns up alone at his owner's house. There is no sign of Ichabod. Many believe the Headless Horseman carried him away. Or did he? One villager heard that Ichabod moved because he was upset about Katrina and the happenings of that night.

In the end, Brom Bones finally marries Katrina. A strange thing happens whenever someone tells him the story of Ichabod. Brom smiles and bursts into laughter when he hears about the broken pumpkin. Maybe, just maybe, there is more to the story.

EXPLORE MORE!

Washington Irving used names of real people for his story. The real Ichabod Crane was a soldier. Katrina Van Tassel was based on a real woman named Eleanor Van Tassel Brush. She is buried in the Sleepy Hollow cemetery.

Ichabod's disappearance becomes a favorite story among the townspeople.

A TIMELESS TALE

Washington Irving didn't come up with the idea of a horseback rider with no head. Old stories from Ireland and Iceland tell of headless riders. The Headless Horseman is most likely based on the German legend of the Wild Huntsman. Washington Irving used his imagination, and real American history, to make a story of his own.

More than 200 years later, people still love "The Legend of Sleepy Hollow." It has been called America's first ghost story. The real town of Sleepy Hollow holds celebrations every Halloween. Maybe you'd like to visit someday!

EXPLORE MORE!

The short story "The Legend of Sleepy Hollow" first came out in a collection of stories by Washington Irving. The book was called The Sketch Book of Geoffrey Crayon. Washington Irving's story "Rip Van Winkle" was in this collection, too.

REAL LANDMARKS OF SLEEPY HOLLOW

Old Dutch Church

Sleepy Hollow Cemetery

Headless Horseman statue

Headless Horseman Bridge

Washington Irving's home, Sunnyside

Around Sleepy Hollow, you can visit real places that honor the legend.

GLOSSARY

American Revolution: The war in which the colonies won their freedom from England.

cannonball: A heavy metal ball shot from a large gun.

cemetery: A place where the dead are buried.

impress: To gain another's interest.

inherit: To get by legal right after a person's death.

jealous: Unhappy and angry because someone has something you want.

legend: A story that has been passed down for many, many years that's unlikely to be true.

prank: A trick or joke done for fun.

saddle: A padded seat used to ride a horse or mule.

whistle: To make a sound by blowing breath through lips or teeth.

witchcraft: The use of sorcery or magic.

FOR MORE INFORMATION

BOOKS

Irving, Washington. *Rip Van Winkle and The Legend of Sleepy Hollow*. Scottsdale, AZ: EDCON Publishing Group, 2020.

Irving, Washington, and Michelle Lemke Riggs. *The Legend of Sleepy Hollow*. Culver City, CA: Living Popups, Inc., 2022.

Keenan, Sheila. *What Is the Story of the Headless Horseman?* New York, NY: Penguin Workshop, 2023.

WEBSITES

Britannica Kids: Washington Irving
kids.britannica.com/kids/article/Washington-Irving/353305
Read more about Washington Irving's life and work.

Pop Goes the Page: Destination: Sleepy Hollow
popgoesthepage.princeton.edu/destination-sleepy-hollow
Learn fun facts and see real photos from the town of Sleepy Hollow, New York.

Stories Podcast: The Legend of Sleepy Hollow
storiespodcast.com/the-legend-of-sleepy-hollow
Listen to a spooky bedtime story of this famous tale.

INDEX